MICHELE CASTAGNETTI

Born in Italy in 1972, Michele Castagnetti
spent his formative years in Rome.
After discovering he had an inclination
for design, Castagnetti studied graphic
design nearby at the Ateneo Creativo in
Milan. At nineteen he came to New York
to further his education. Four years later
he received a Bachelor's Degree in Fine
Arts at the Fashion Institute of Technology.

Michele Castagnetti has won awards
in art direction, design, photography
and filmmaking.

Castagnetti art series have appeared in
numerous galleries and exhibitions.
His art is regularly published in the art
magazine Rojo. Castagnetti's fine art
photography was also published in
Graphis Best of Photography in 2003.

Michele Castagnetti has won awards in
art direction, design, photography and
film. Castagnetti's award-winning
experimental short film "I close my eyes
and walk away" was on the shortlist for
an Academy Award® in 2010.

Castagnetti art series have appeared
in numerous galleries and exhibitions;
recently in Los Angeles at Fresh 2014
curated by the maverick Coagula curator
Mat Gleason and at Gallery 825 curated
by the Los Angeles Times art critic
David Pagel.

The series Femme Fatale represents a
synthesis of the traditional and the modern.
The experimental technique used utilizes
both photography and painting. Pigment
and polymer colors have been applied
onto traditional photographic prints.
The spontaneous reaction of all the media
used helps create each unique piece.

Through his work, the artist has also
supported a number of charitable
organizations, including WriteGirl,
Chrysalis, Step Up Women, TreePeople
and Amnesty International.

FEMME FATALE

The tension between reality and illusion, between
tradition and modernity, is Michele Castagnetti's
theme, his expression seamlessly joining two
disciplines, those of photography and painting.
He uses the female archetype, that of the
dangerous and intuitive woman in a vision of life,
yet acutely aware of death. The clothing, the
jewelry and the surroundings are simply elements
to decipher the women's complex personalities.
His fascination for sensuality, sharp color and
bold intensity generates an impulse to decipher
the secrets locked inside the subject.

The beauty of the feminine is central to whatever
love and immortality we're sensing. Mythological
influences permeate Castagnetti's work, allegorical
representations of the seductive woman, the
erotic fascination, the secrets of the unconscious,
the labyrinth of the soul. If you allow yourself to
get lost in the gaze of one of his "femme fatale"
series, the intensity of the subject reveals a swift
semblance of womankind's mystery.

Layla Revis
Contributing Editor · Art+Living Magazine

FEMME FATALE

MICHELE CASTAGNETTI

Helen
Polymer and pigment color
on gelatin silver print, mounted on canvas
48 X 60 inches (121.9 X 152.4 cm)

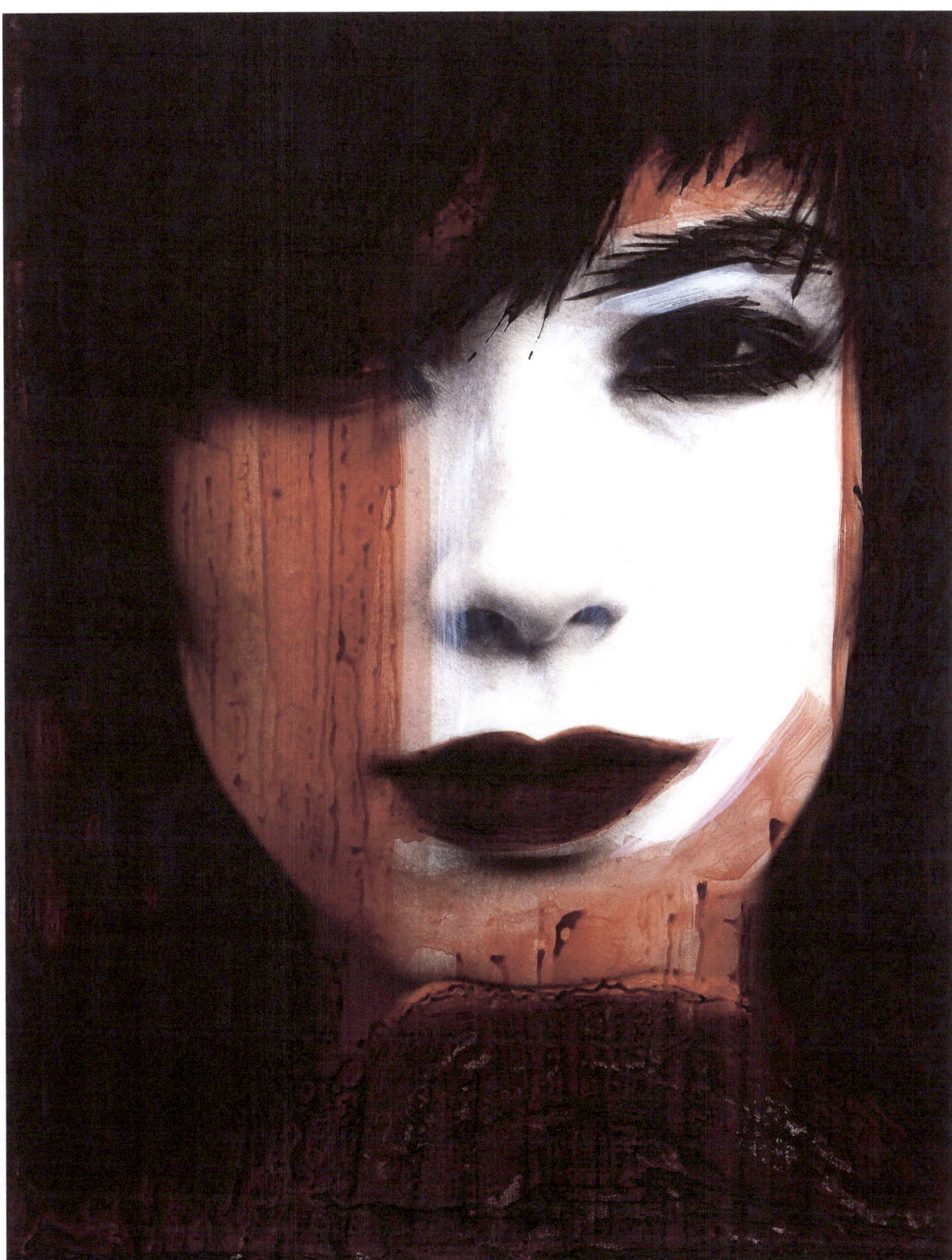

René
Polymer and pigment color
on gelatin silver print, mounted on canvas
48 X 60 inches (121.9 X 152.4 cm)
Collection of Candice Scott, Palos Verdes

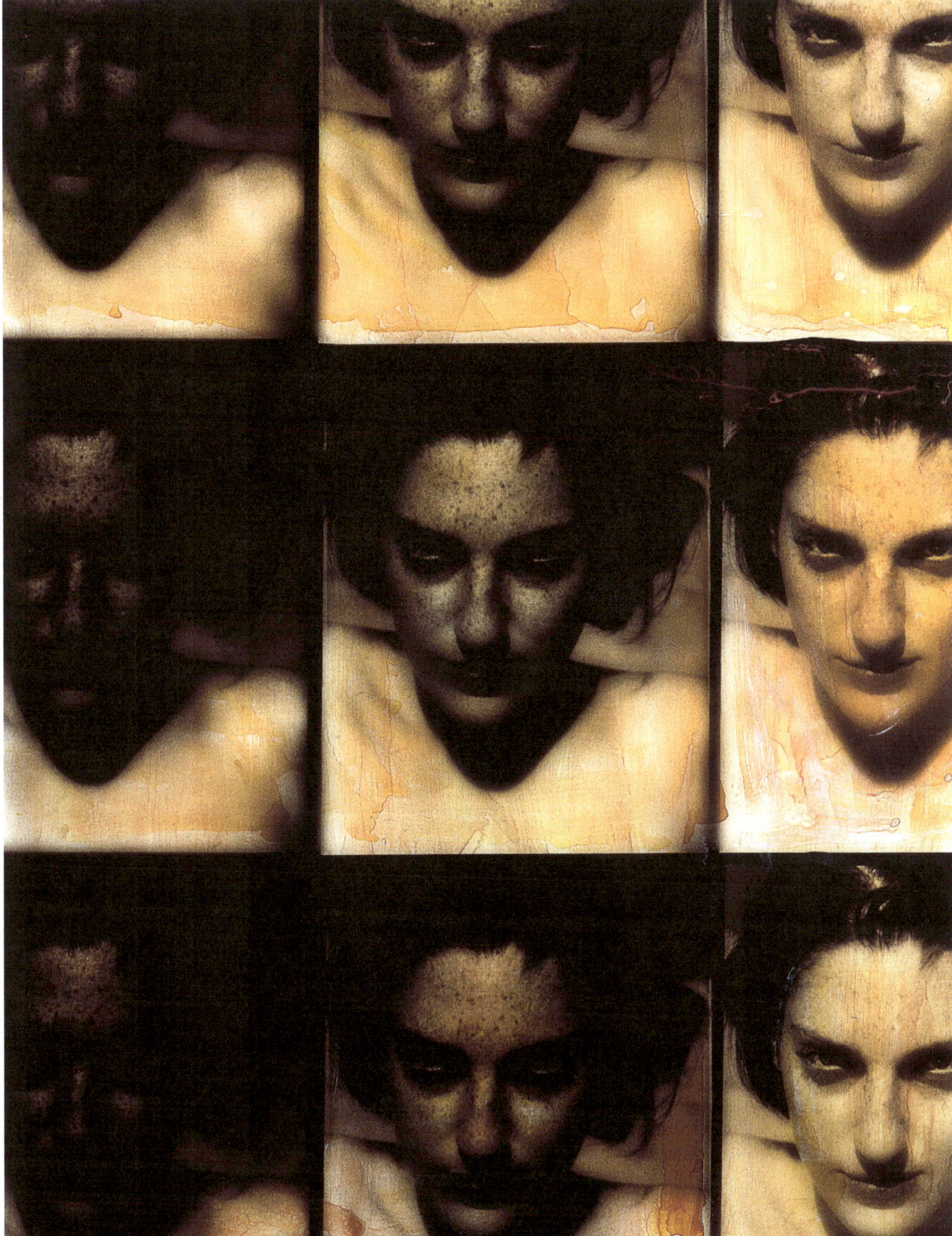

Igea
Polymer and pigment color
on gelatin silver print, mounted on canvas
48 X 36 inches (121.9 X 91.4 cm)
Collection of Mamaly Reshad, Los Angeles

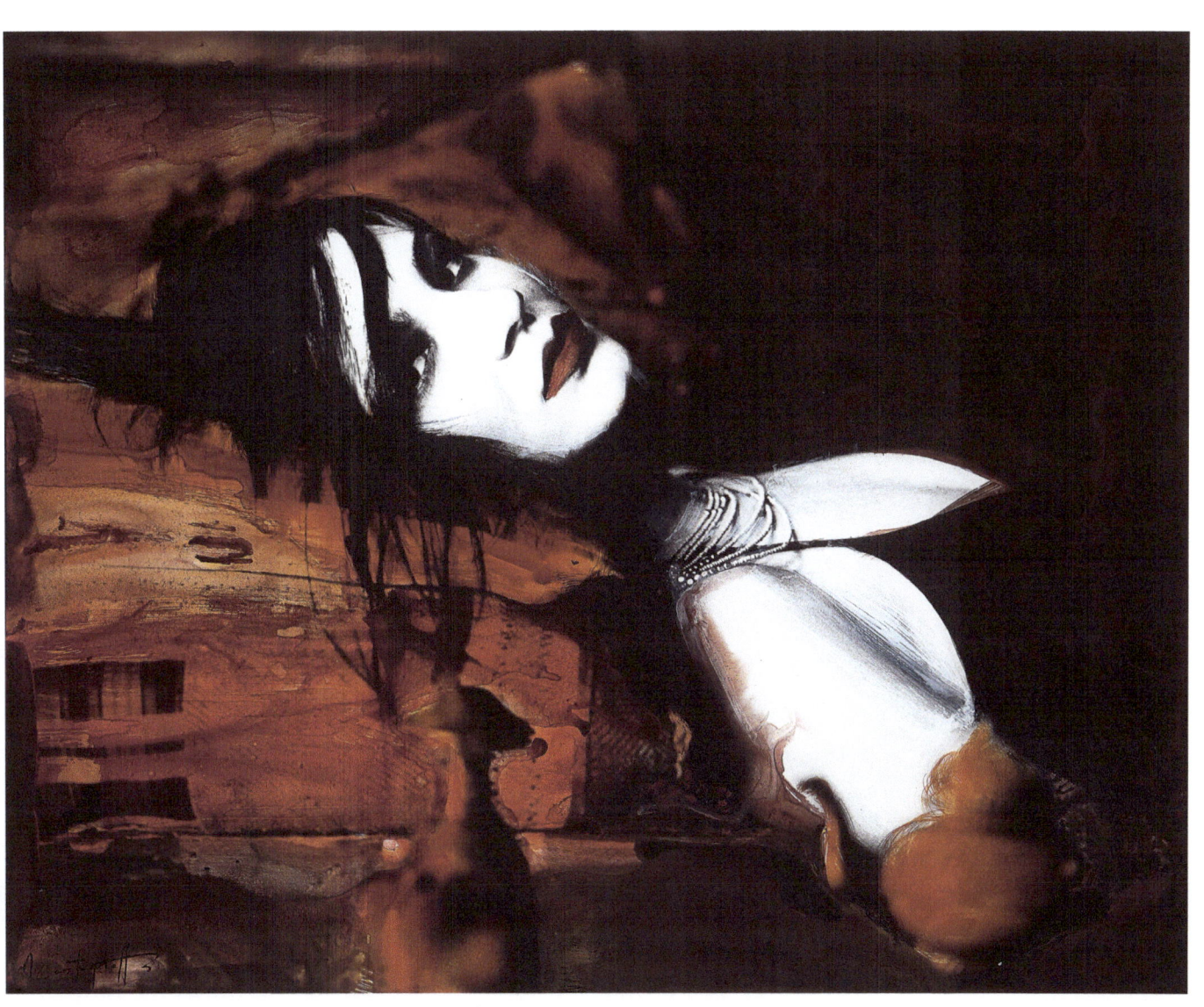

Nana
Polymer and pigment color
on gelatin silver print, mounted on canvas
40 X 60 inches (101.6 X 152.4 cm)
Collection of Mamaly Reshad, Los Angeles

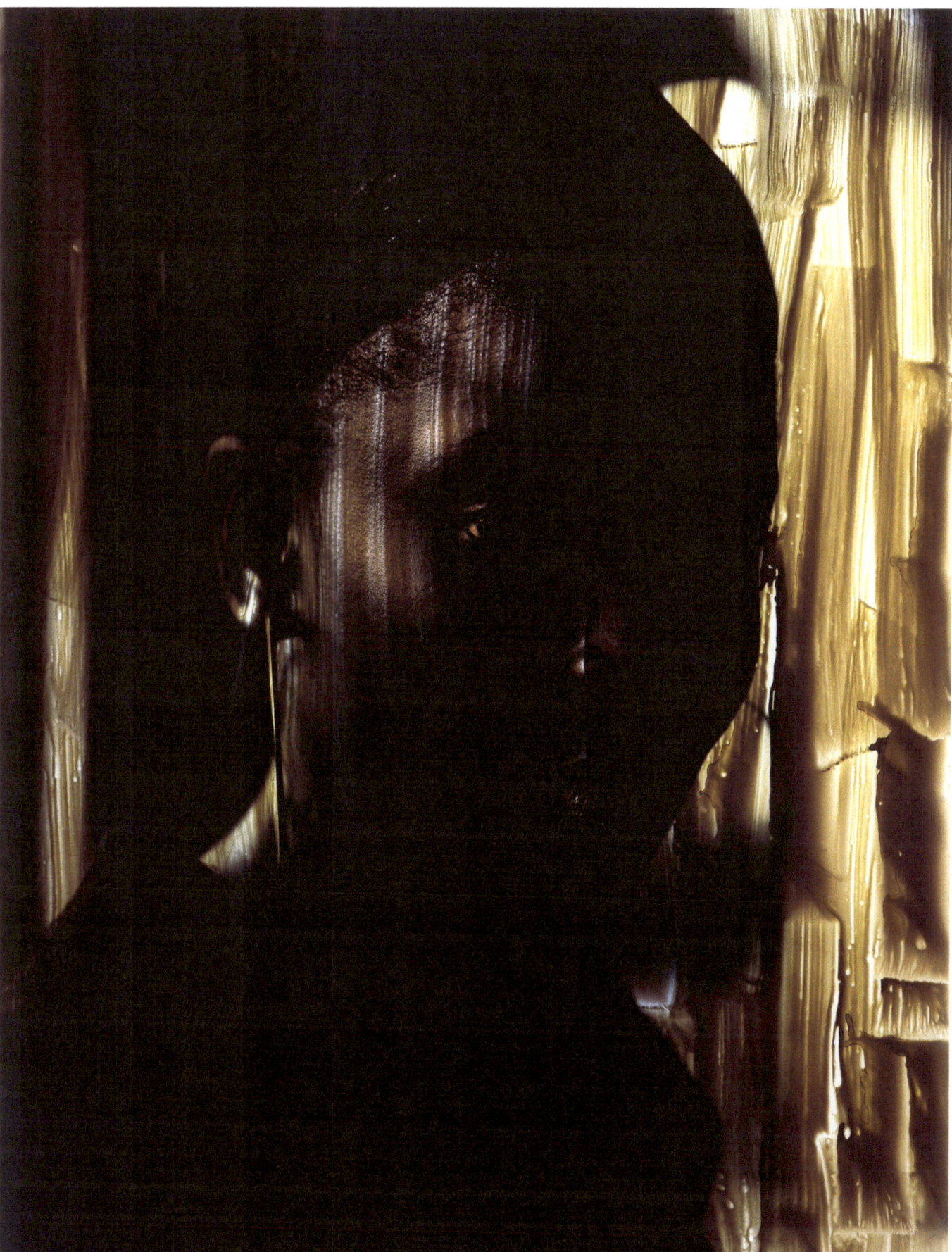

Cecilia
Wallpaper, polymer and pigment color
on gelatin silver print, mounted on canvas
48 X 60 inches (121.9 X 152.4 cm)

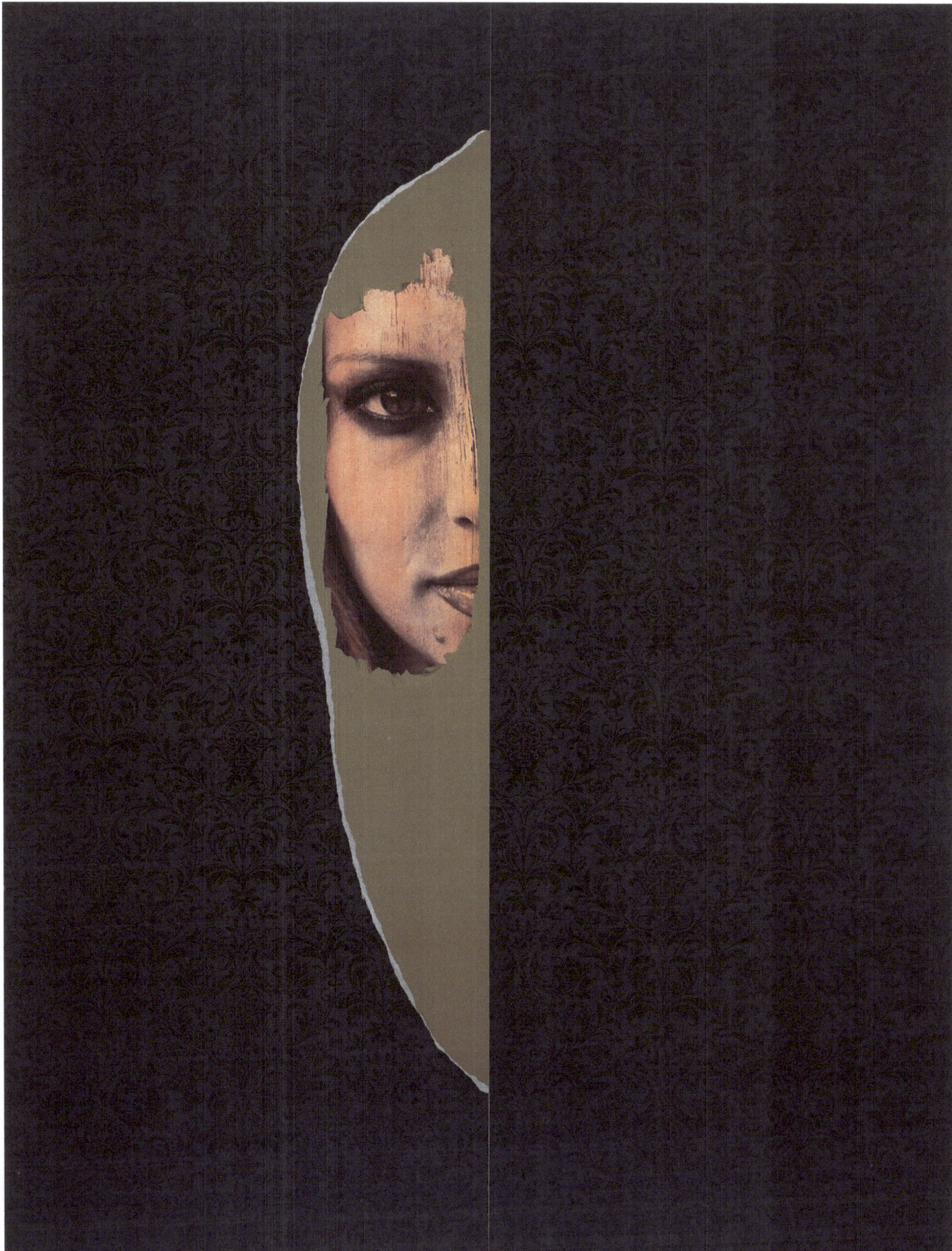

Claire
Printed wallpaper, polymer and pigment color
on gelatin silver print, mounted on canvas
36 X 48 inches (91.4 X 121.9 cm)

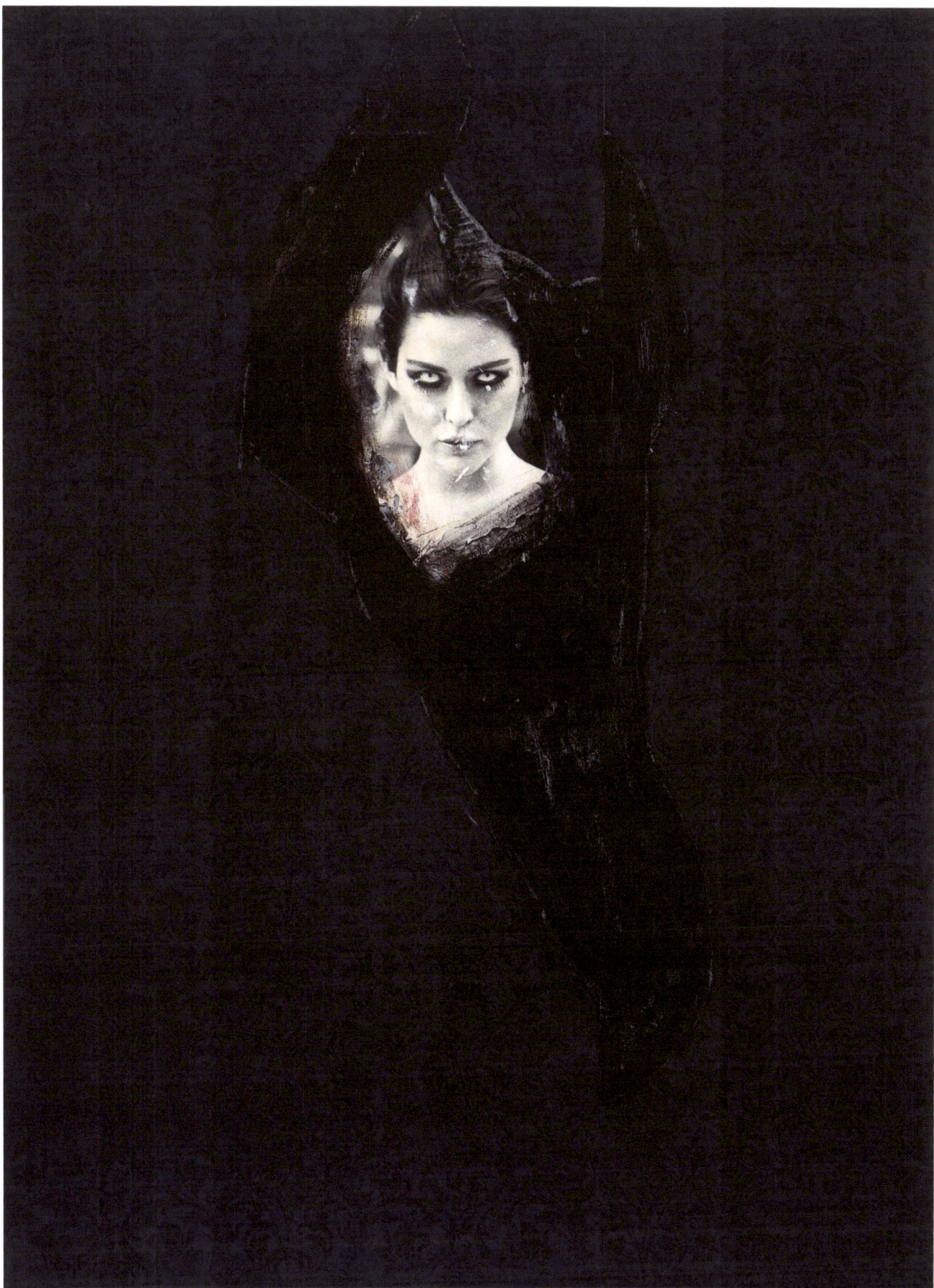

Solange
Printed wallpaper, polymer and pigment color
on gelatin silver print, mounted on canvas
48 X 60 inches (121.9 X 152.4 cm)

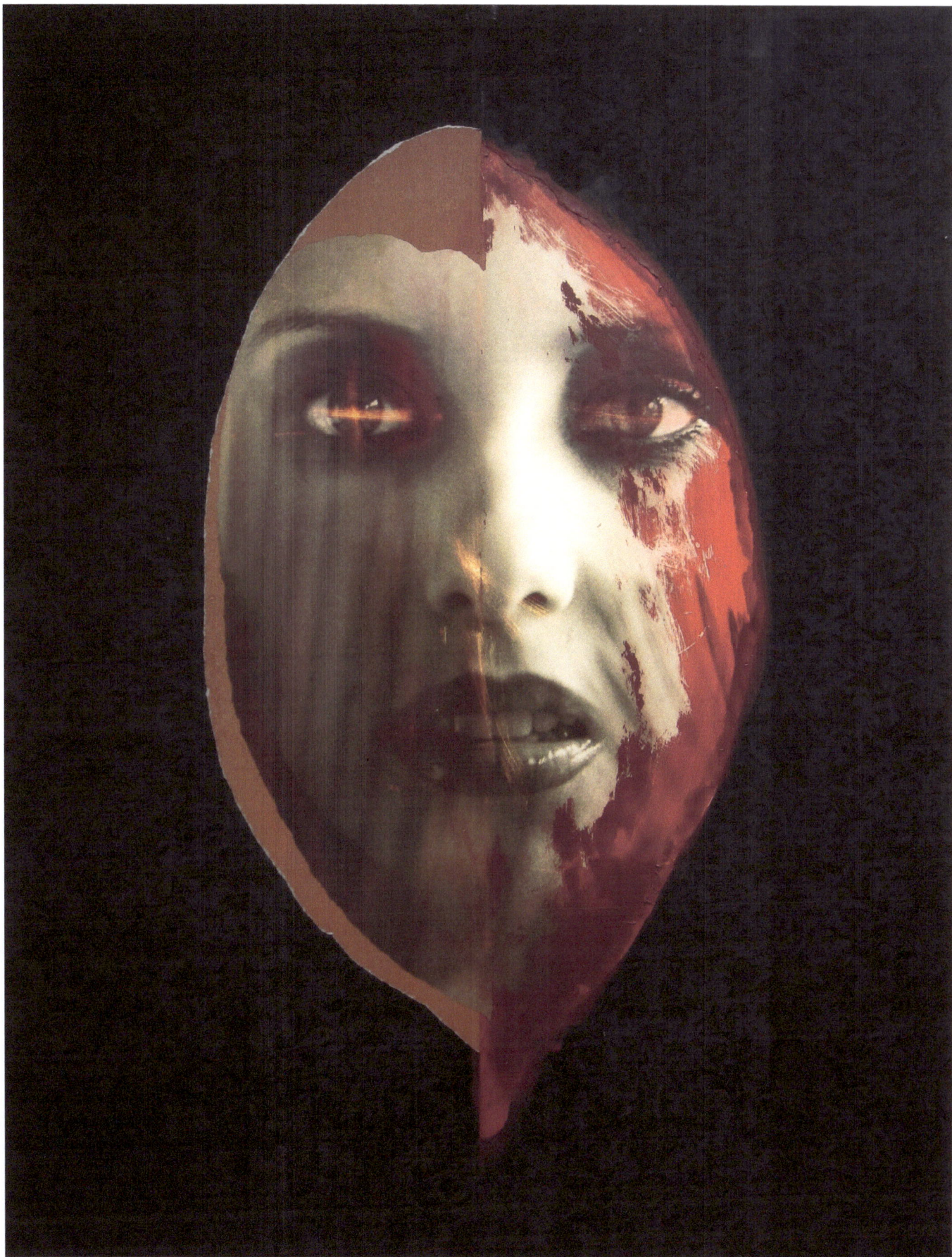

Kemp
Printed wallpaper, polymer and pigment color
on gelatin silver print, mounted on canvas
48 X 60 inches (121.9 X 152.4 cm)
Donated to APLA, Los Angeles

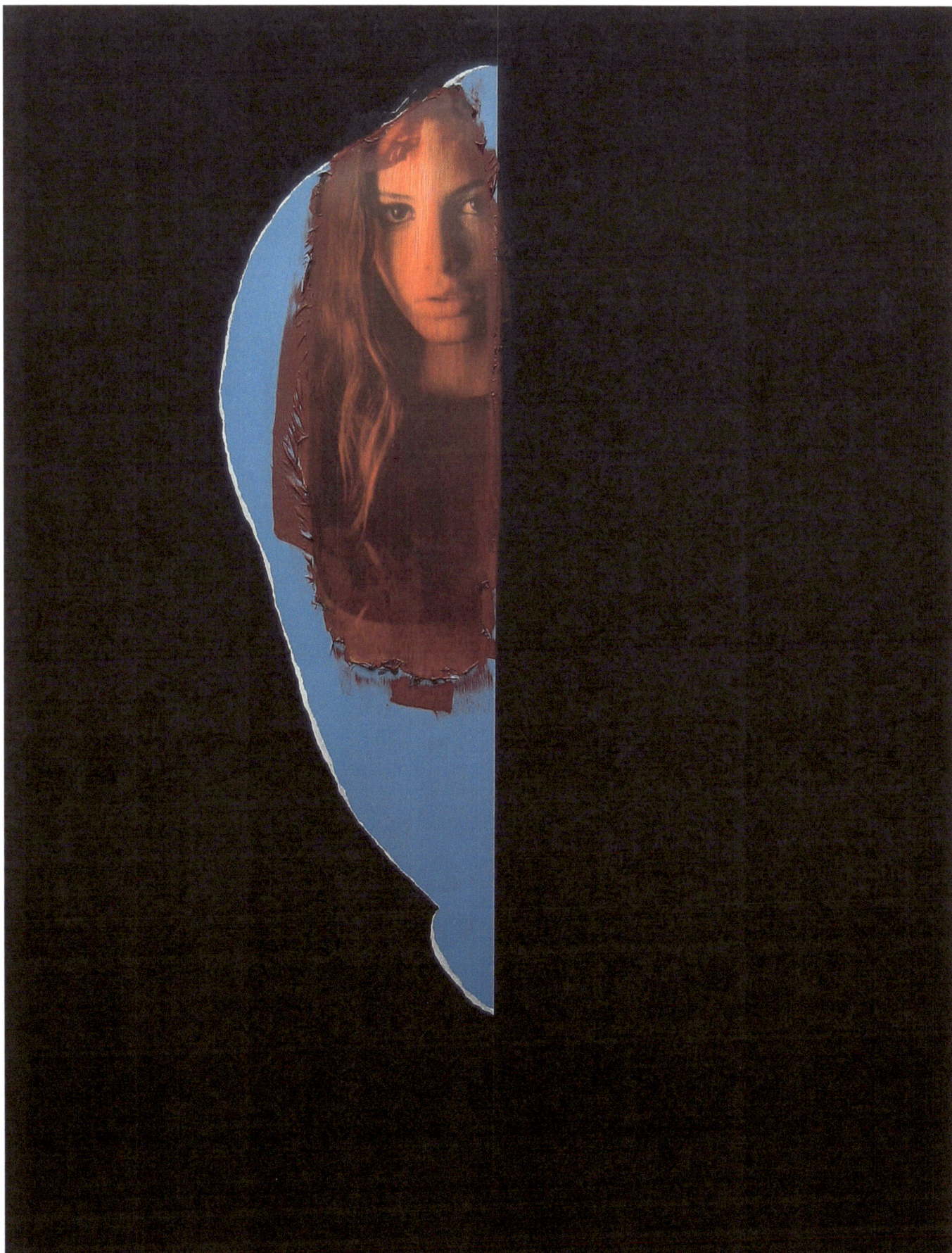

Lisette
Polymer and pigment color
on gelatin silver print, mounted on canvas
48 X 60 inches (121.9 X 152.4 cm)
Collection of Steven Krause, New York

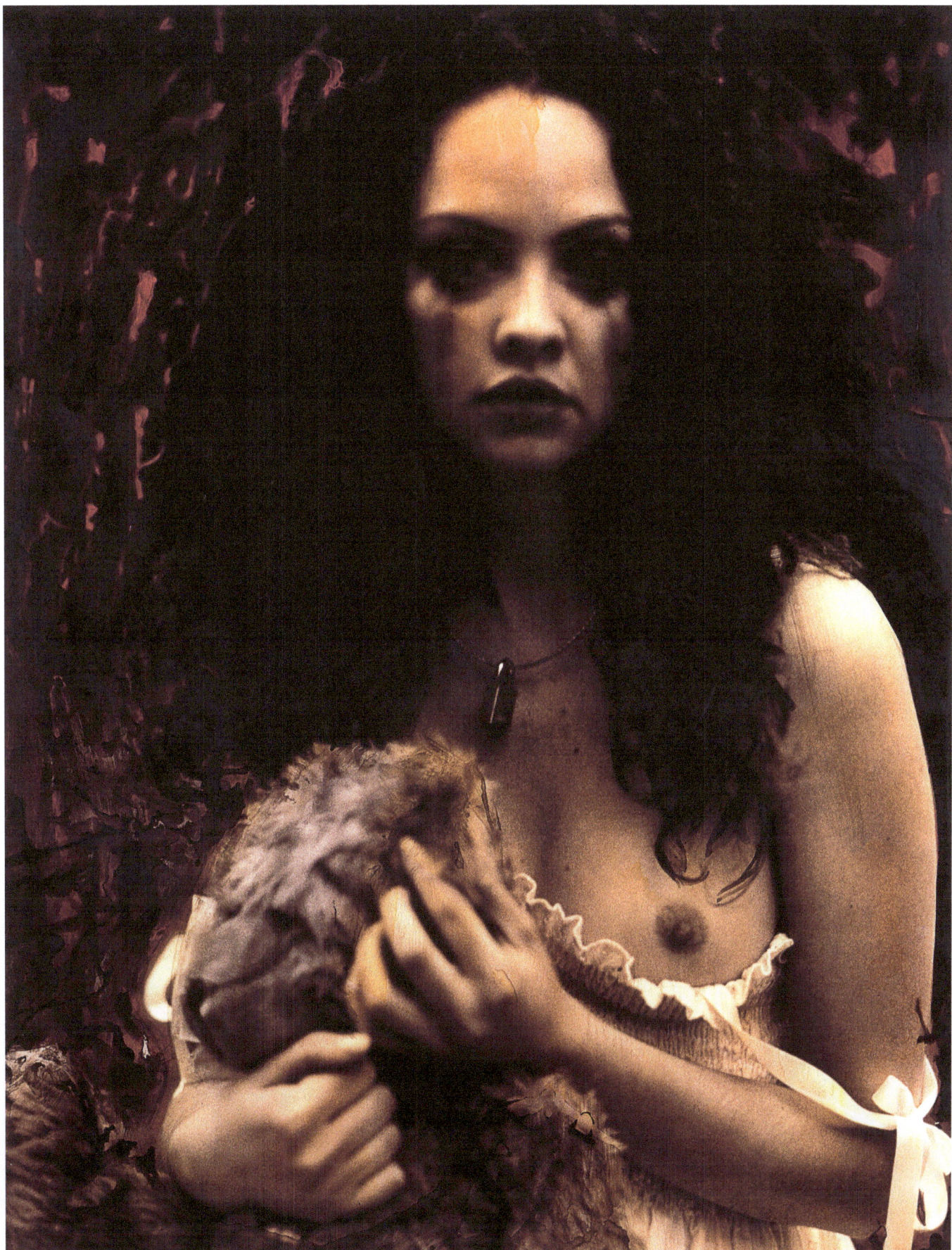

M.
Polymer and pigment color
on gelatin silver print, mounted on canvas
48 X 60 inches (121.9 X 152.4 cm)

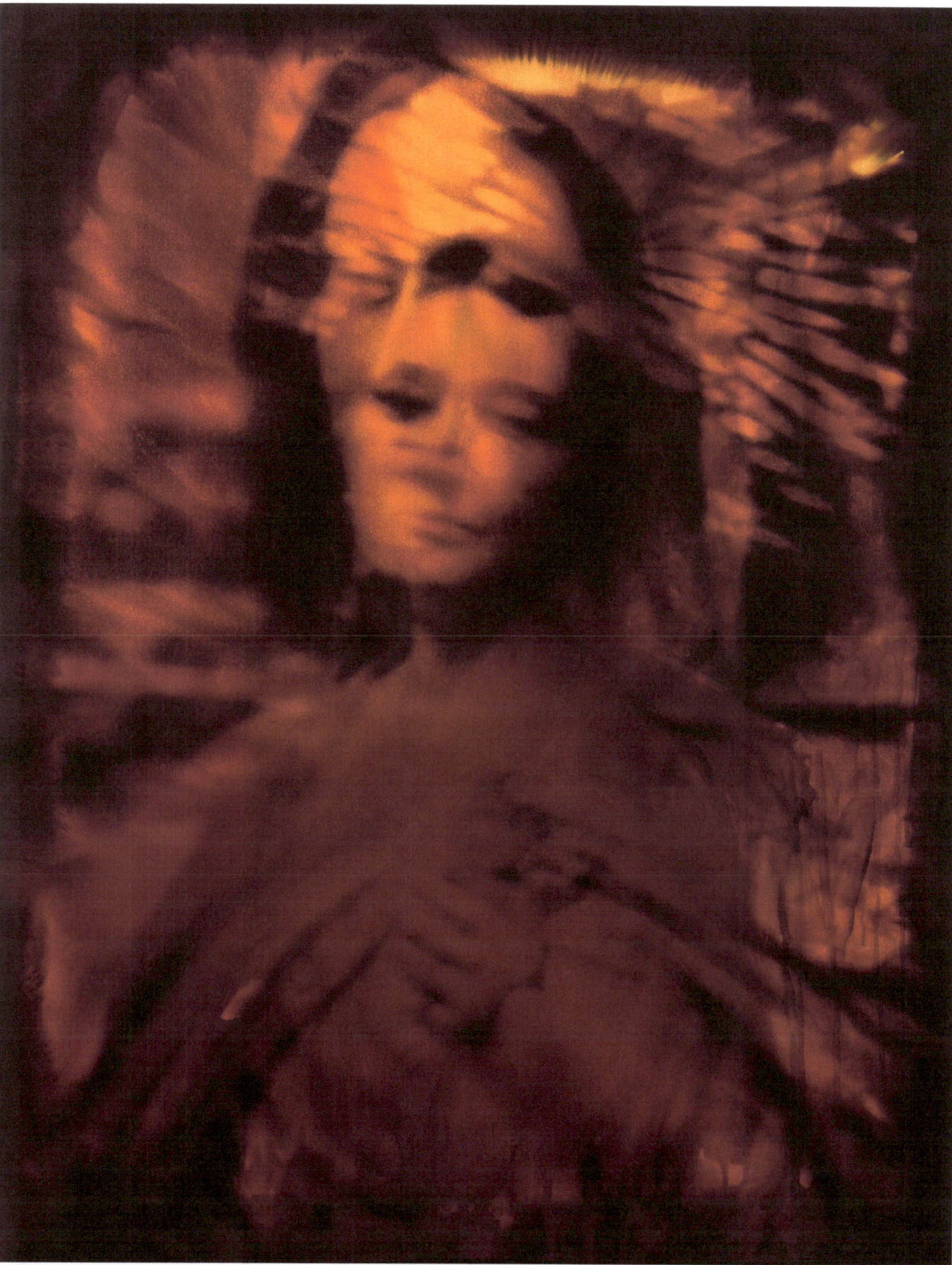

Claire
Polymer and pigment color on
gelatin silver print, mounted on canvas
40 X 60 inches (101.6 X 152.4 cm)
Collection of Mitsuo Yasuda, Tokyo

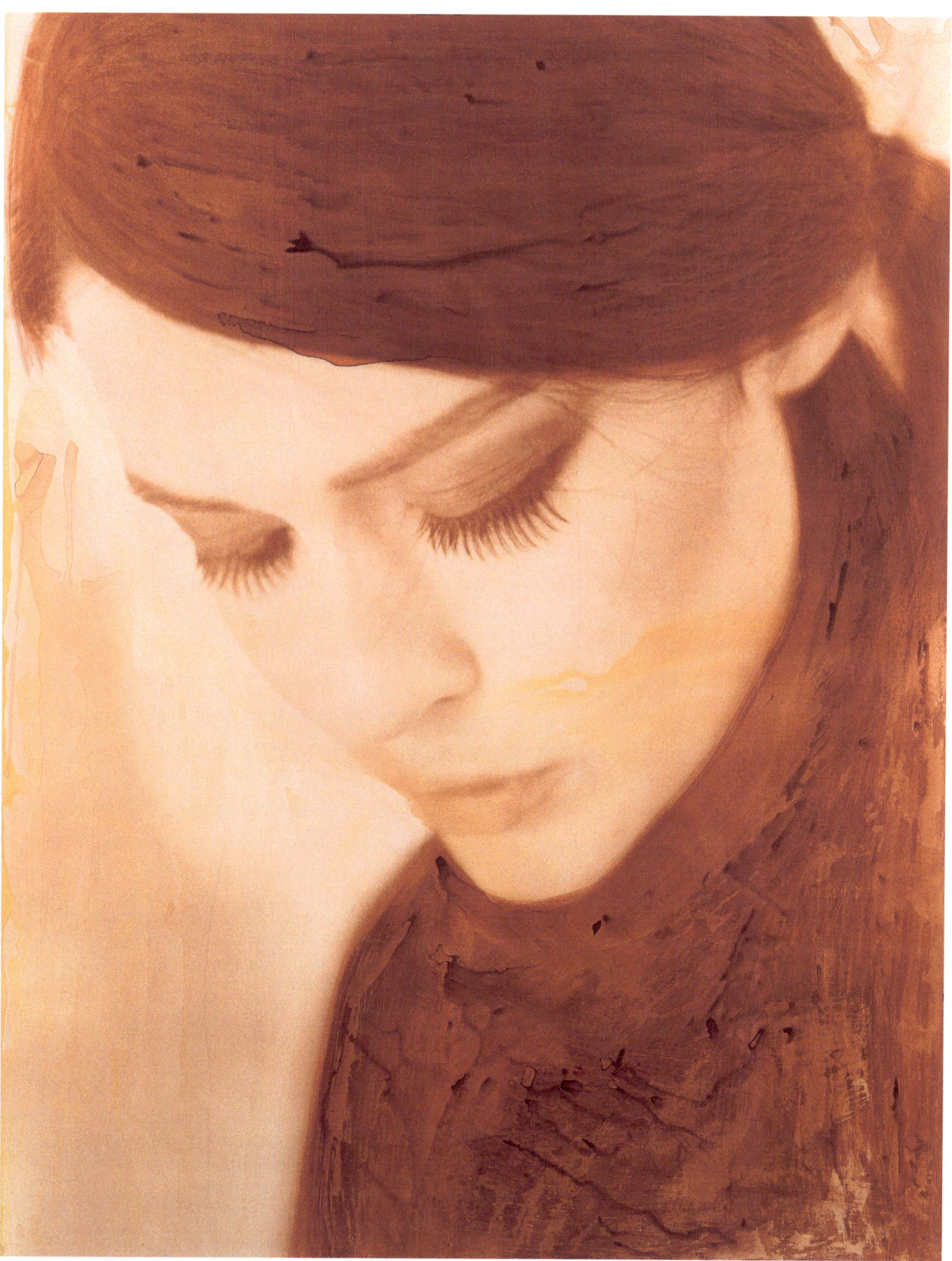

Midgi
Polymer and pigment color
on gelatin silver print, mounted on canvas
40 X 60 inches (101.6 X 152.4 cm)
Collection of Sandra Lugo, New York

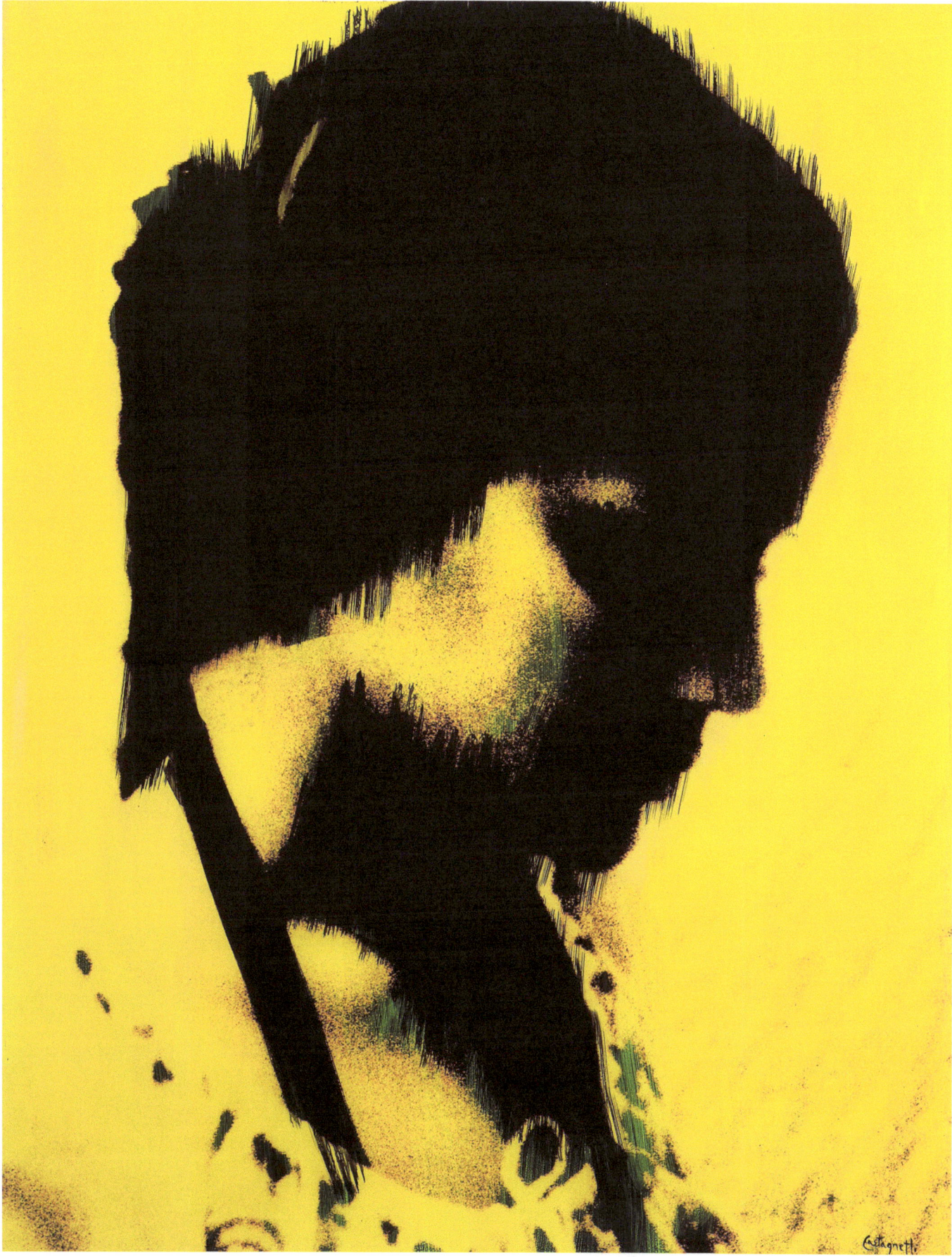

Amy
Polymer and pigment color on
gelatin silver print, mounted on canvas
36 X 48 inches (91.4 X 121.9 cm)
Collection of Amy Pesner, Los Angeles

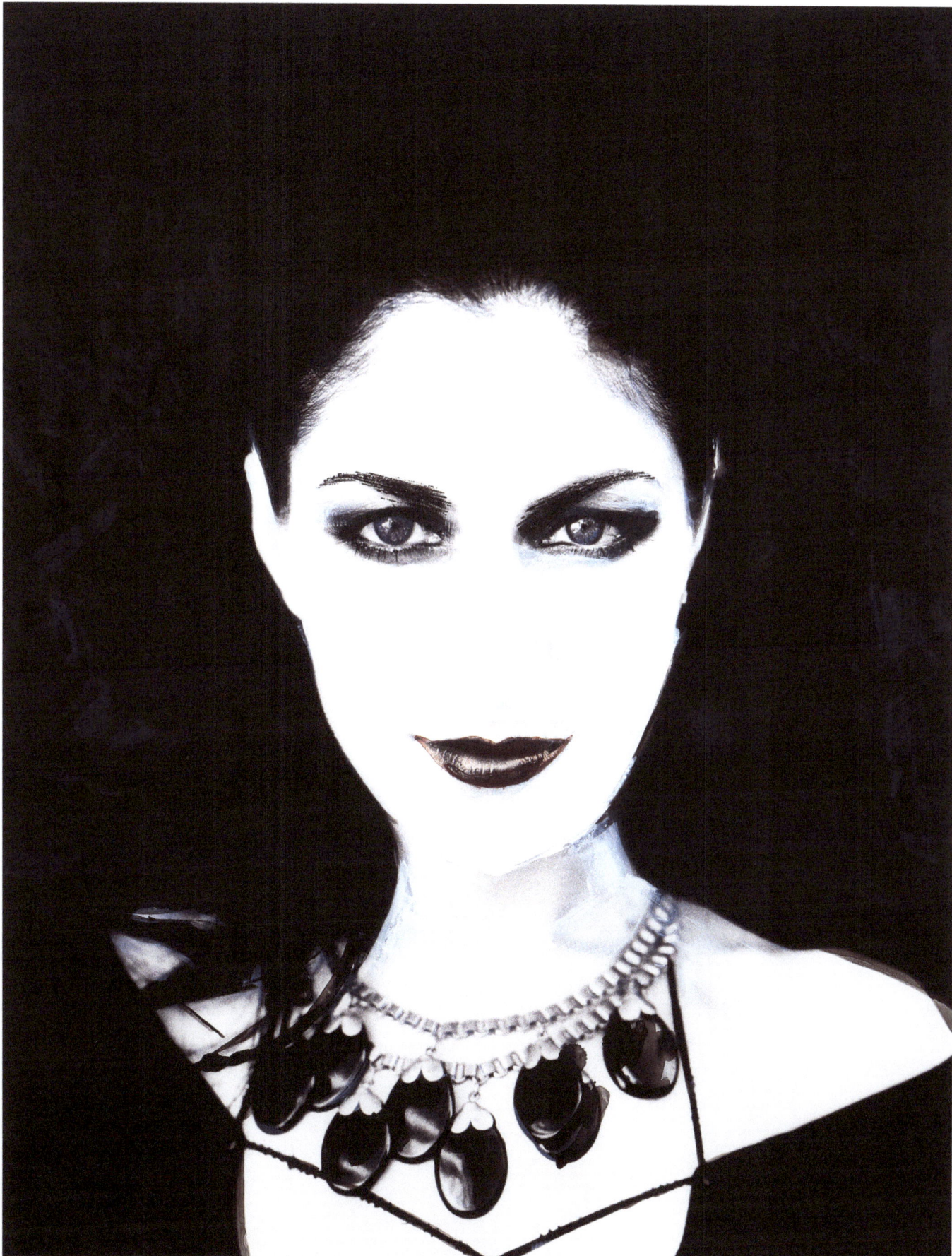

Natasha
Polymer and pigment color
on gelatin silver print, mounted on canvas
48 X 60 inches (121.9 X 152.4 cm)

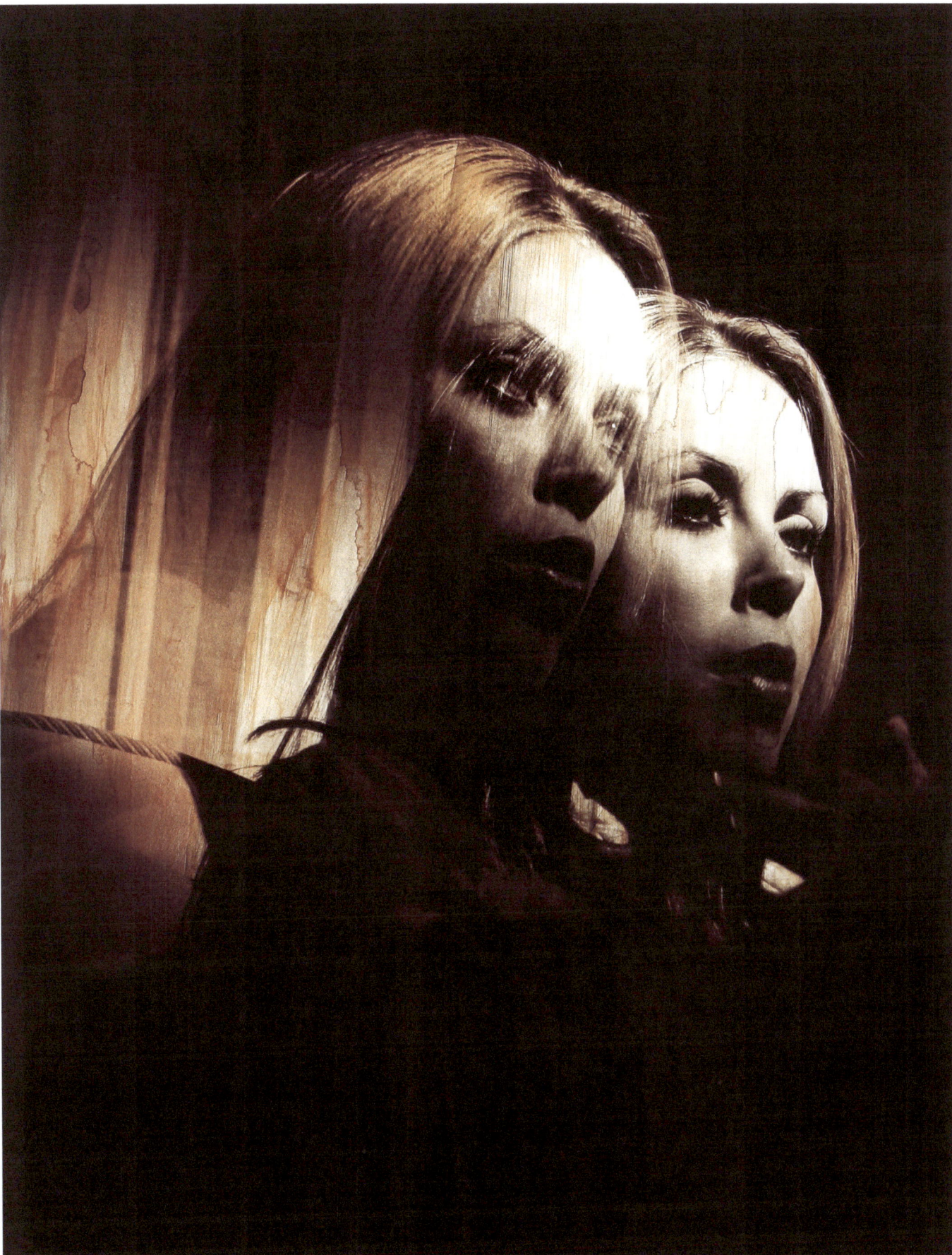

Erika
Polymer and pigment color
on gelatin silver print, mounted on canvas
48 X 60 inches (121.9 X 152.4 cm)

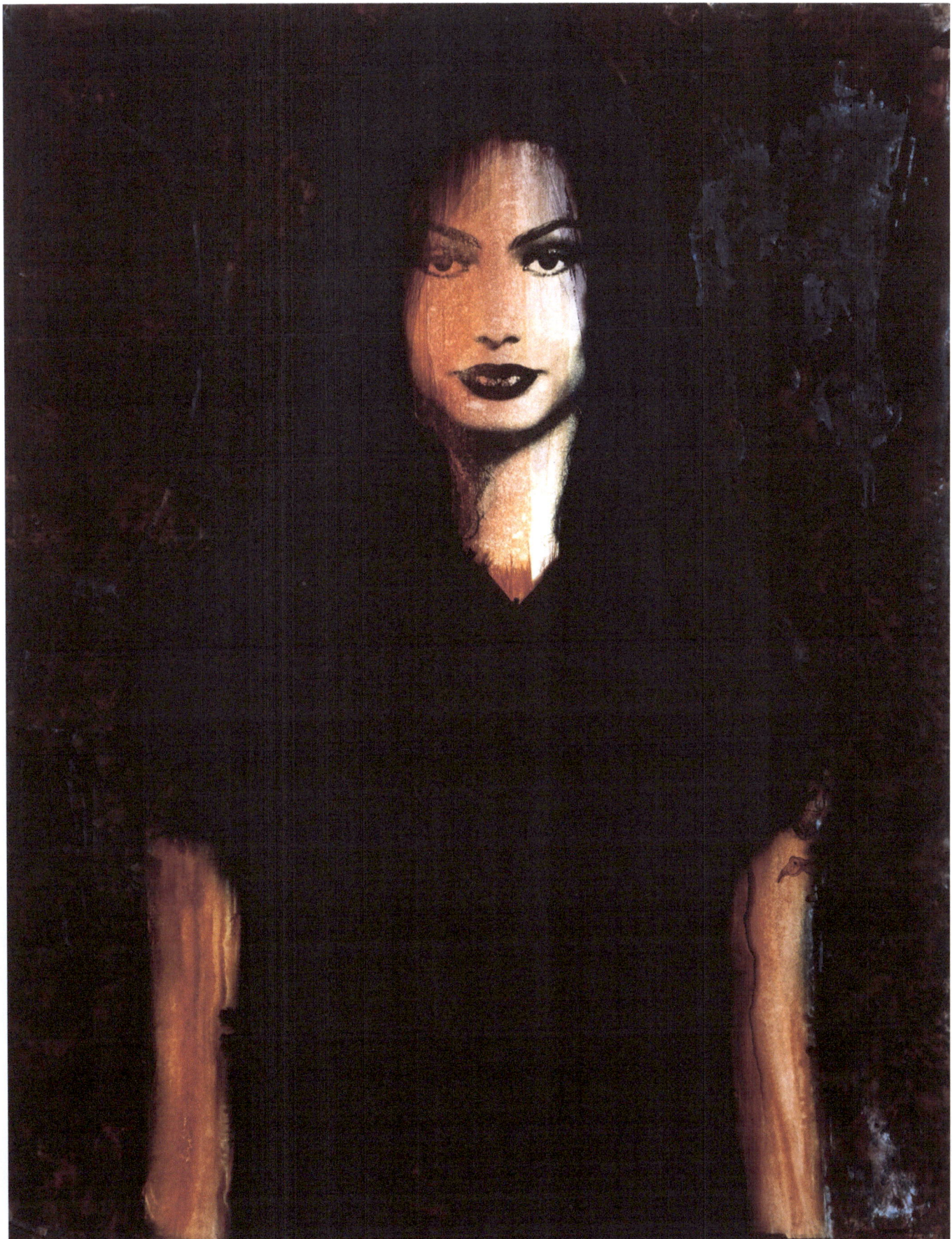

Acqua
Polymer and pigment color
on gelatin silver print, framed
40 X 60 inches (101.6 X 152.4 cm)
Collection of Norma Hunt-Allen, Los Angeles

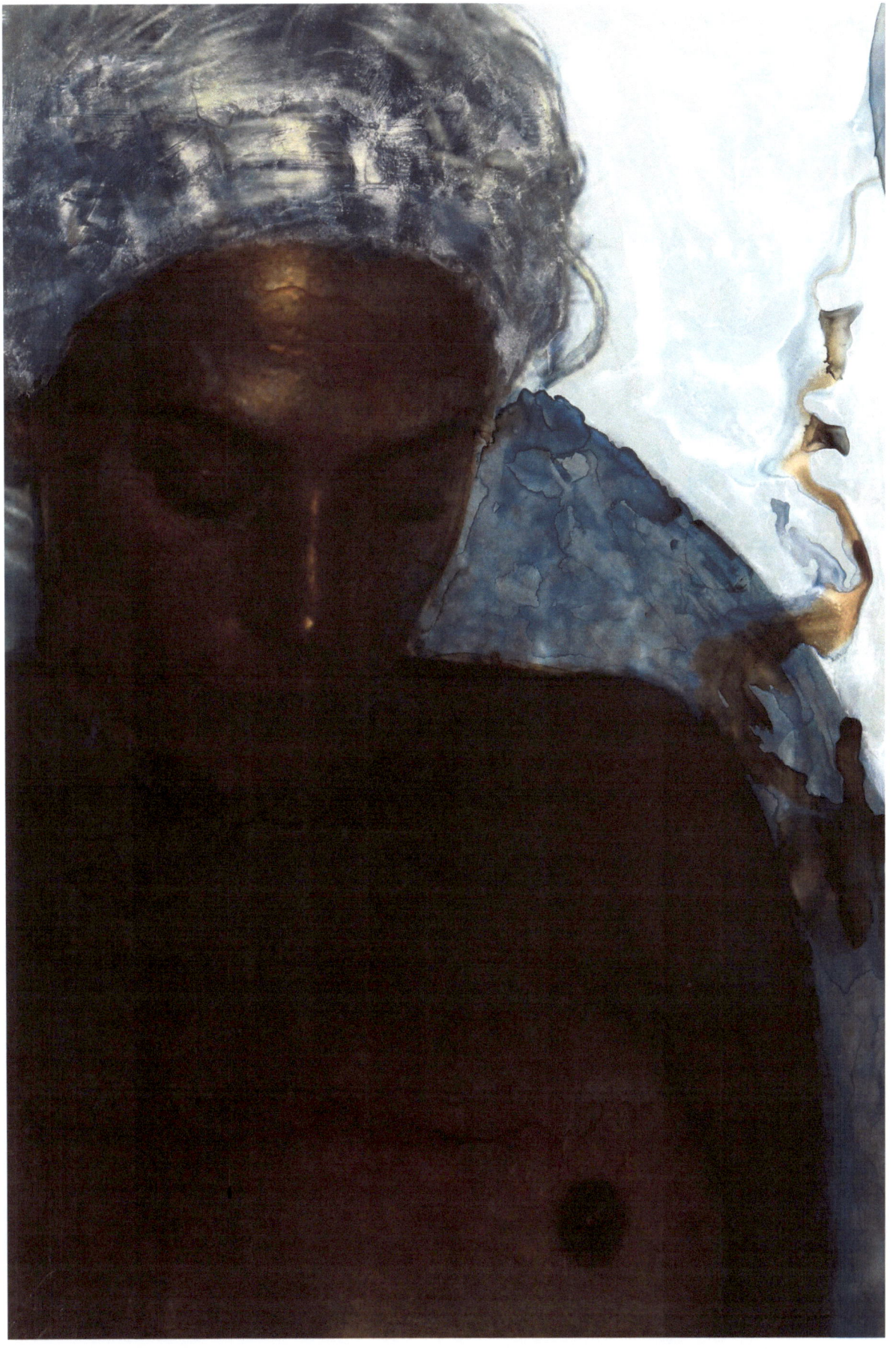

Sandra
Polymer and pigment color
on gelatin silver print
48 X 60 inches (121.9 X 152.4 cm)

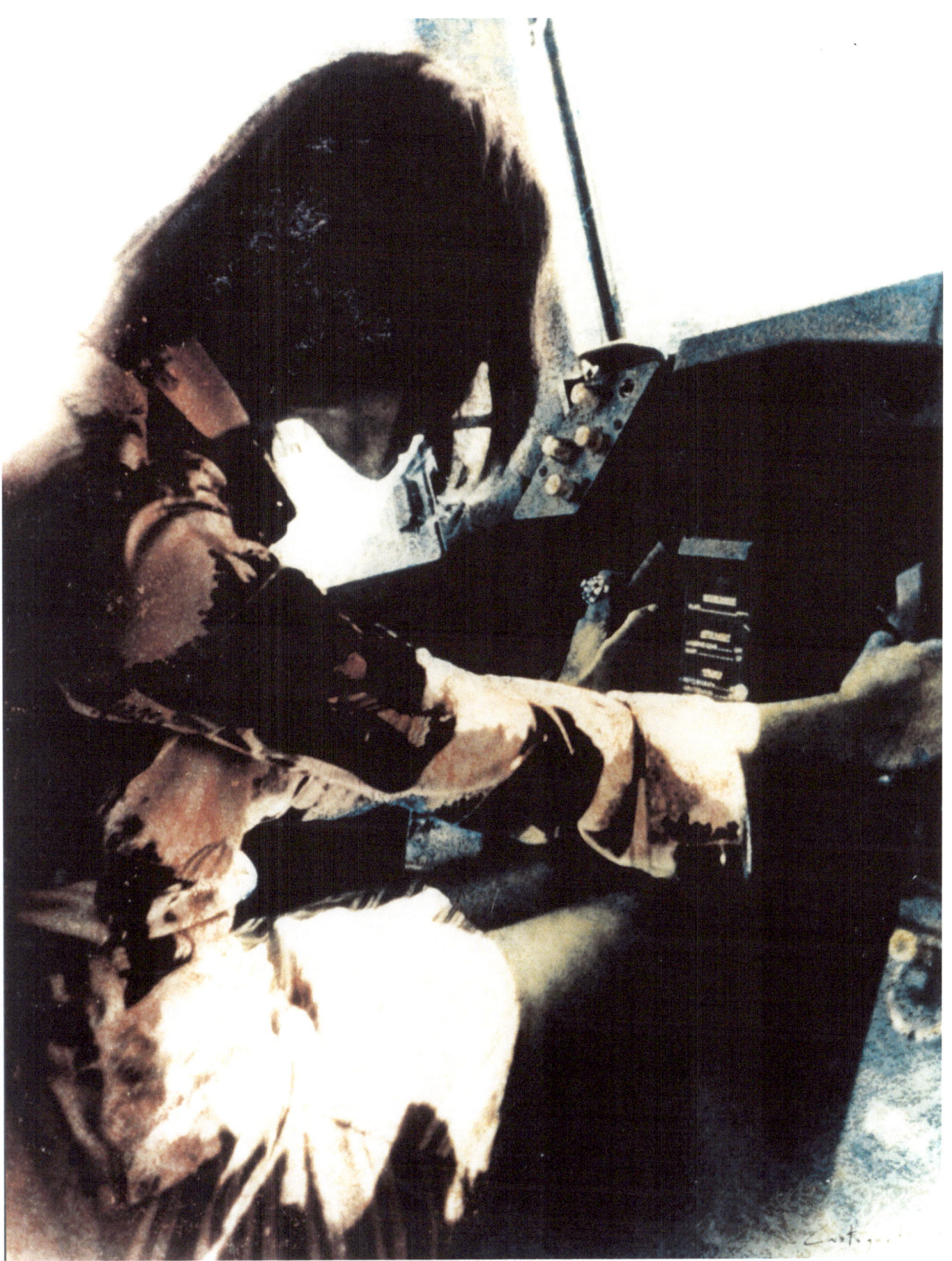

Takako Tsuji
Polymer and pigment color
on gelatin silver print mounted on canvas
48 X 60 inches (121.9 X 152.4 cm)
Collection of Harvey Kaner, Los Angeles

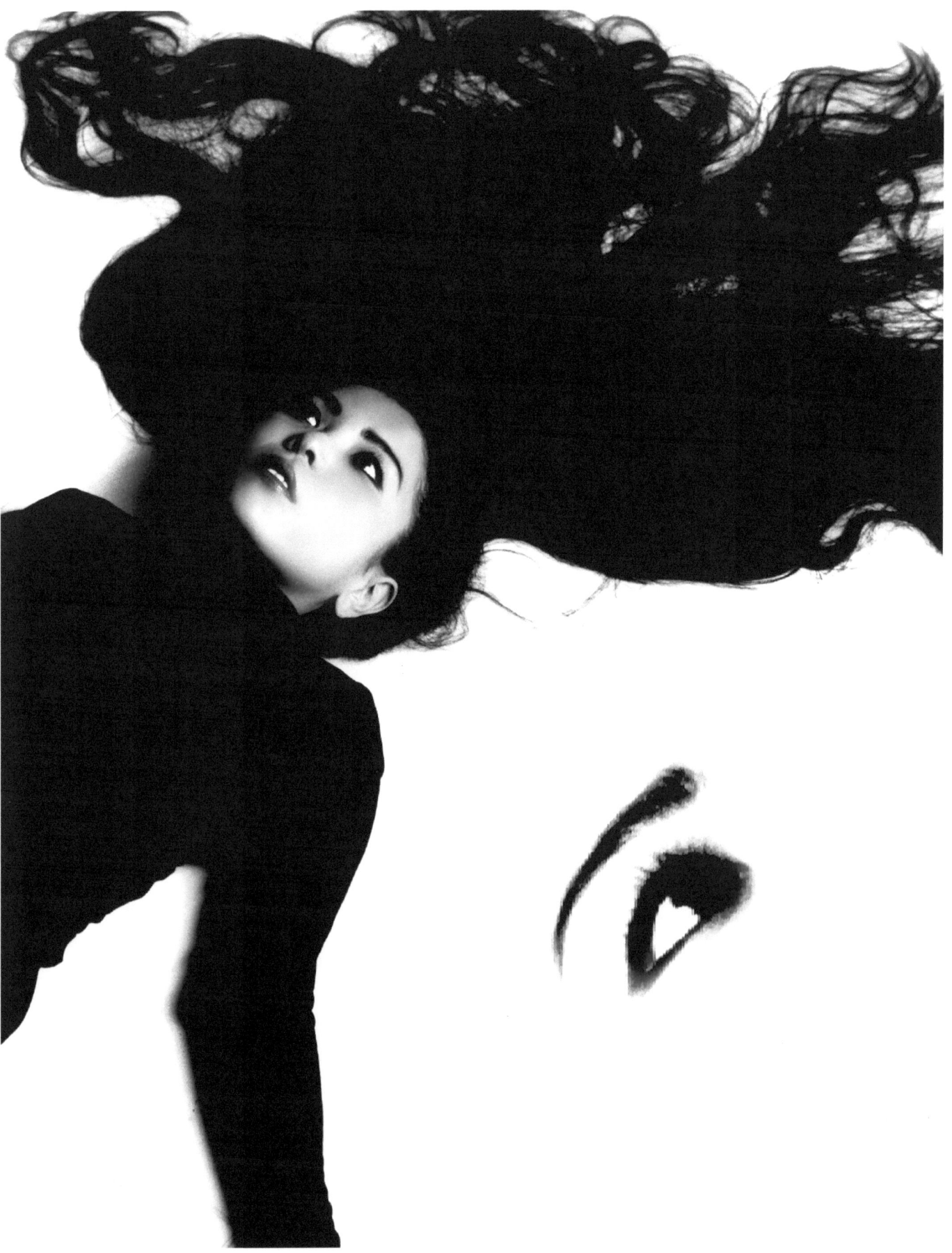

Kirke
Polymer and pigment color
on gelatin silver print mounted on wood panel
40 X 60 inches (101.6 X 152.4 cm)
Collection of Queens College Art Center, New York

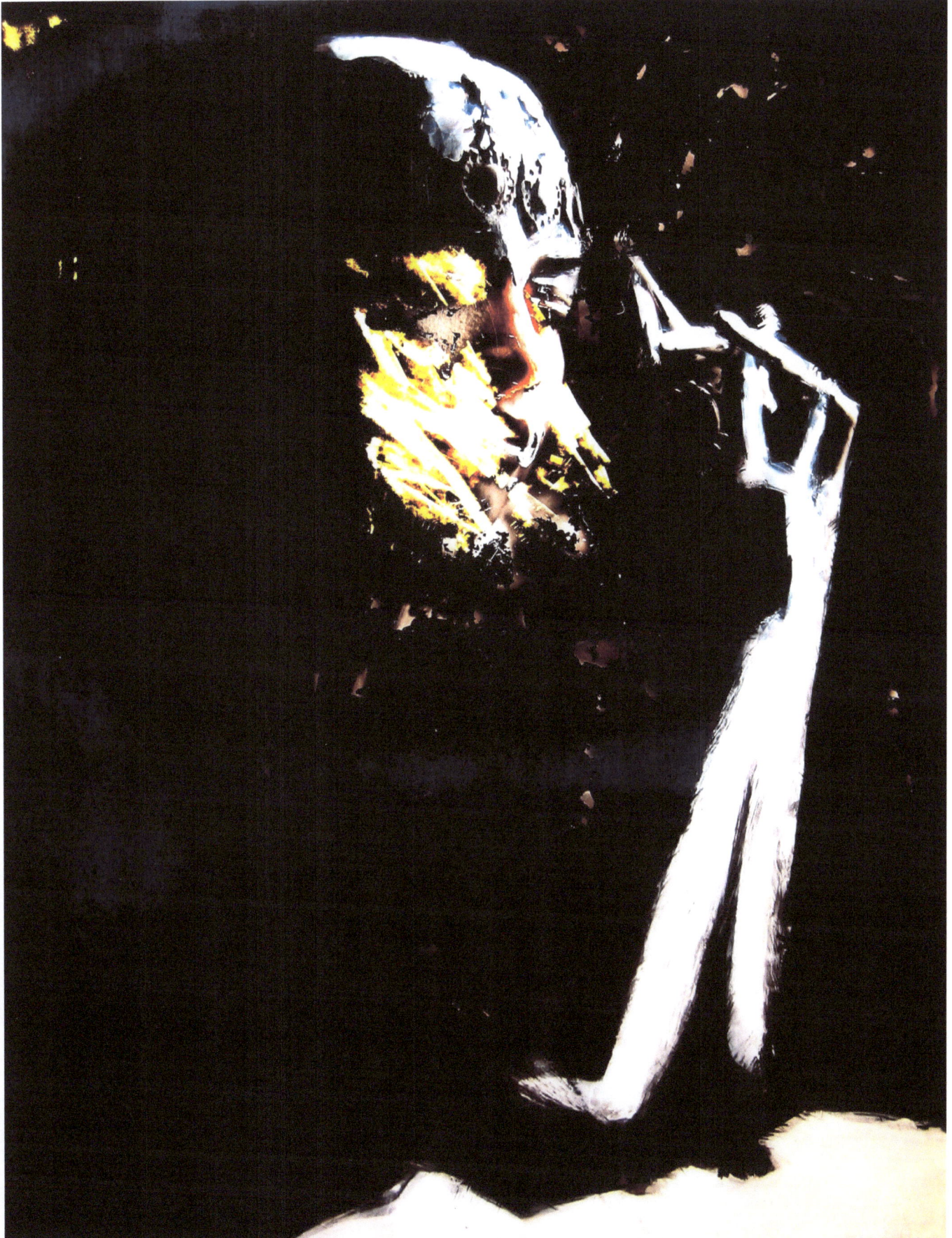

Jackline
Polymer and pigment color
on gelatin silver print
11 X 14 inches (28 X 35.5 cm)

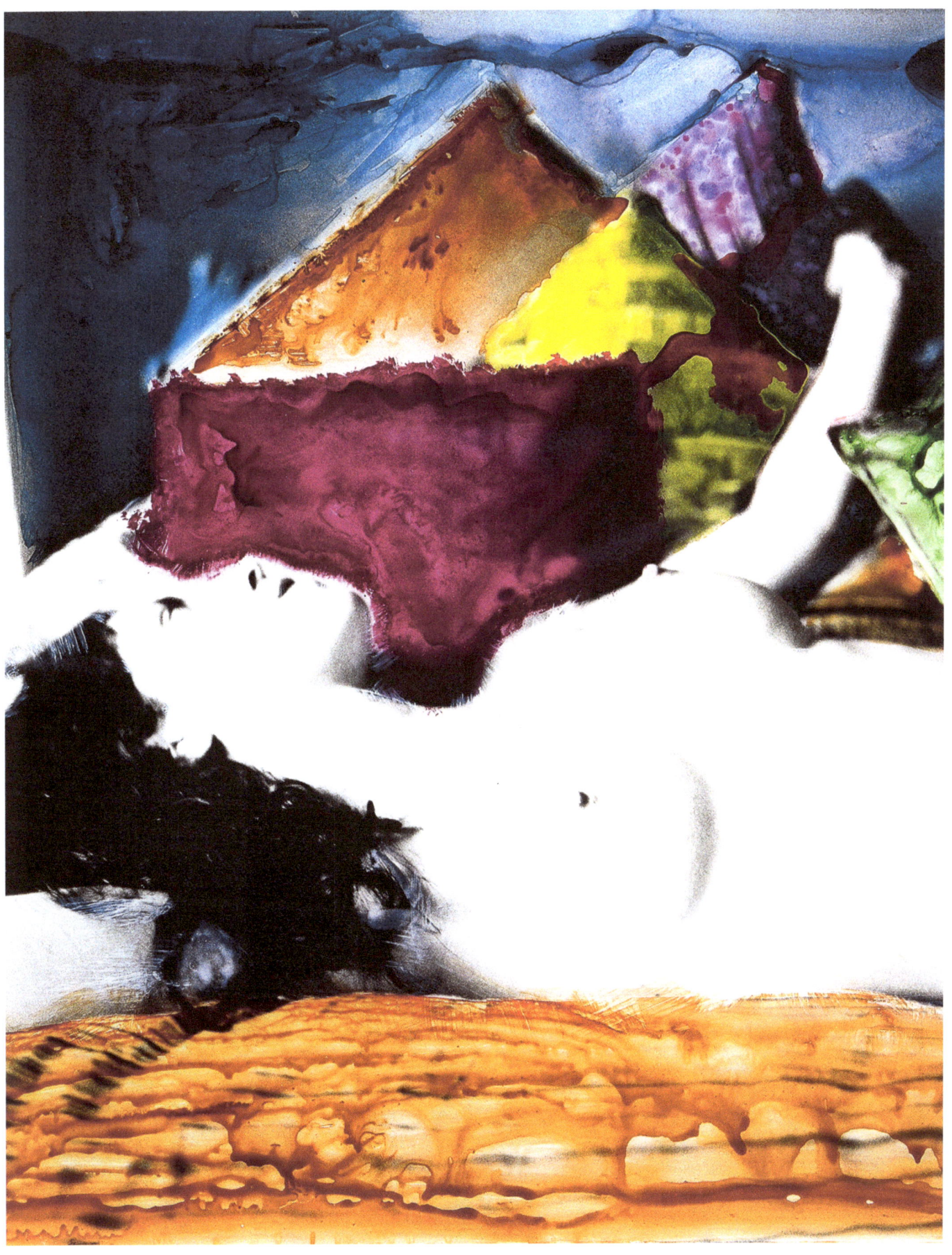

www.ingramcontent.com/pod-product-compliance
Lightning Source LLC
Chambersburg PA
CBHW050903180526
45159CB00007B/2769

9 781530 136902